Presents for Jack and Billy

Story by Jenny Giles

Illustrations by Betty Greenhatch

Dad went away on a big plane.

"Come and look at the photo on the computer, Billy!" said Jack.

"I can see Dad! And I can see a truck!"

"I can see a red **helicopter!**"

said Billy.

Jack said,

"The red helicopter

is for you, Billy.

And the blue truck

is for me."

"Look!" shouted Billy.

"Here comes Dad!"

Dad said, "The helicopter is for you, Jack.
And the truck is for you, Billy."

"Thank you, Dad," said Jack and Billy.

Jack said,

"Here is the helicopter, Billy."

Billy said,

"Here is the truck, Jack."

"Thank you, Billy," said Jack.

"Thank you, Jack," said Billy.